Making M

Cameron Macintosh

Contents

A Part of Our Lives

Music is an important part of our lives. It brings us together and makes our lives more fun.

Every culture has its own music. In some places, music has been a part of the culture for thousands of years.

Musical Instruments

Most music is made with musical **instruments**.

Do you play an instrument?

bass guitar

piano

There are lots of different musical instruments that you can try!

recorder

violin

There is one special instrument that everyone can use. Your voice is an instrument too!

You can use your voice anywhere. You can sing by yourself or with other people.

A group of singers is called a **choir**. Singing in a choir is a fun way to learn about music.

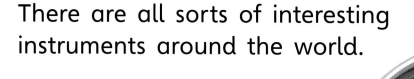
Instruments Around the World

There are all sorts of interesting instruments around the world.

Some children play the ankle bells. The bells ring as they move their feet.

Some children play the clapsticks. The clapsticks make a sound when they are tapped together.

Some children play the panpipes. They blow across the top of the pipes to make different sounds.

Some children play tribal drums. The drums are played by hand rather than with drumsticks.

Some children play the chapchas. These are rattles made from the toenails of goats!

Ways to Play

There are lots of different ways to play music. Some people play music that has been written down.

Each dot or circle in the music is a **note** to be played. The music tells the player which note to play and how long to play it for.

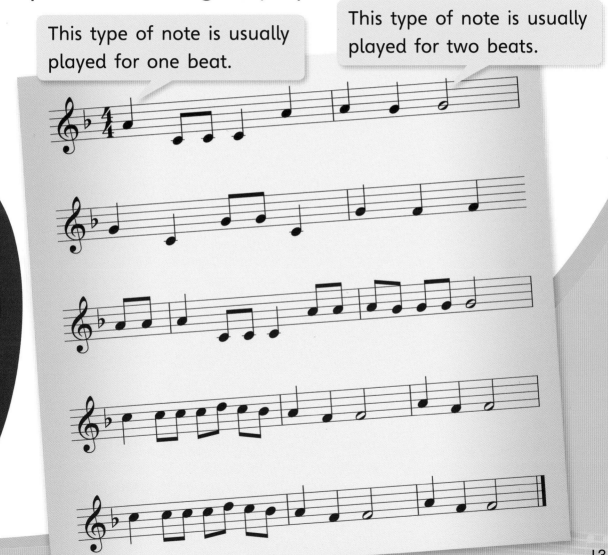

Some people don't write down music. They play music they have learned by **memory**.

Some people write their own music
or make it up as they go!

It's Good for Us

Singing or playing a musical instrument is good for us too!

Our brains get lots of exercise when we make music. This is good for our memory.

Singing or playing music in a group also helps us to work well with other people.

We Can All Make Music

Even if you don't have an instrument, you can still make music.

You can clap your hands or stomp your feet.

You can hum or sing or whistle.

Everyone can have fun when they make music!

Make Your Own Drum

Drums are lots of fun to play. Let's make one!

You will need:

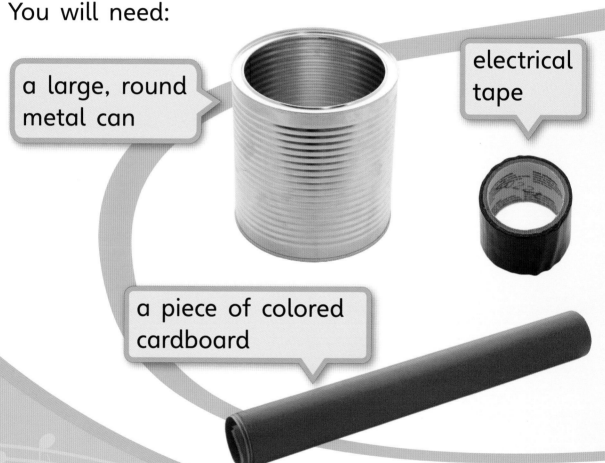

a large, round metal can

electrical tape

a piece of colored cardboard

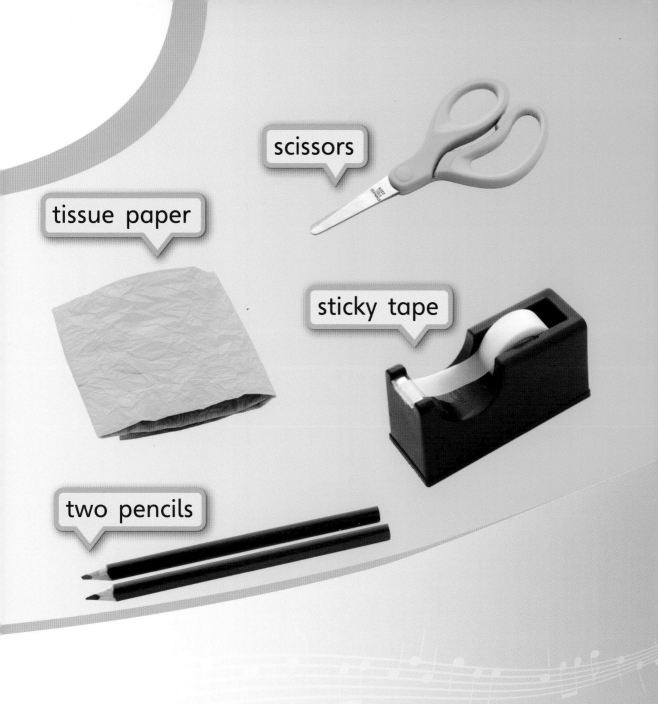

scissors

tissue paper

sticky tape

two pencils

21

1. Cover the top of the tin can with strips of electrical tape.

2. Cut the cardboard to fit around the can.

3. Wrap the cardboard around the can, and stick it on with the sticky tape.

4. Decorate your drum. You can use anything you like.

5 Roll the tissue paper into two balls. Tape it to the ends of the pencils. Now you have drumsticks.

Your drum is ready to play!

Glossary

choir a small or large group of people who sing together

instruments devices used to make musical sounds

memory the ability to remember things

note a musical sound